W9-AGP-182

THE JOY OF SERVICE!

Bringing Service Excellence To The World Through Your Work

by

Ron McCann

Business Services Consultant

and

President
Service Operations Systems, Inc.

as told to Joe Vitale

THE JOY OF SERVICE! Copyright 1989 by Ronald R. McCann and Joseph G. Vitale. All rights reserved.

No part of this book may be reproduced or transmitted in any form or by any means electronic or mechanical including photocopying and recording, or by any information storage and retrieval system, without written permission from the authors.

ISBN 0-9617549-2-3

Library of Congress Catalog Card Number: 89-90863

This book is available at a special discount when ordered in bulk quantities.

The authors are available for seminars, interviews and speaking engagements.

Published by Service Information Source Publications, 10707 Corporate Drive, Suite 101, Stafford, Texas 77477.

Printed in the U.S.A.
First Edition

"No matter whether you manufacture, grow, produce, distribute, or sell, you are 'in service'."

--Paul Hawken,
Growing A Business

ACKNOWLEDGMENTS

We want to publicly thank Royce McCann, Tim White, Richie Ford, Sandi Moncure, Scott Hammaker, Michael Collier, Jim King, Larry Andrews, Susan McCann, Marian Vitale, Rich Thayer, Frank Todaro and Tim Marvins for reading and reviewing the early drafts of this book. Their comments and suggestions served us in creating a clearer and more powerful manuscript.

Sandy Butler provided constant support, made typesetting arrangements and provided detailed editorial feedback.

We also want to acknowledge you, the reader, for purchasing this book. Your act has proven you have a desire to give service to the world. It's our intention that *The Joy of Service!* inspire the reader to recognize and acknowledge the feeling of joy you experience when you serve or are served.

Yours in service,

Ron McCann

Joe Vitale

SERVICE FROM JOY

Our children are born into this revival,
Unselfish serving *from* joy, not *for* joy.
      We never serve for profits.
There is no war.
We are busy serving each others' needs.
      It is a busy peace.
People Caring, People Sharing, People Being Human.
Our talents used to serve mankind.
      Thank you, God, that there are those who need.
We are always related, but our relationship is active only
While we are serving each other.
      Love occurs during service.
Thanks for serving those that serve others that serve me.
Before I serve, I accept personal responsibility
      To give you legendary service.
Service feels like pride surrounded by humility,
      Unselfish giving.
Service is extra ordinary---beyond our expectations.
      We continue to raise our expectations.
Allowing myself to be served is to the server
      As serving is to me.
      Let the children feel the *Joy of Service!*

*This book was written to leave you at the beginning of your future.
The commitments you make, the action you take will speak out to
the world where you stand in the revival of service in America.*

Ron McCann

CONTENTS

For Our Children

The Joy of Service!

Chapter One

WHY SERVE?

or,

The *Joy* of Service!

"To love what you do and feel that it matters---how could anything be more fun?"

--Katherine Graham

I began my career in the service business over twenty years ago. Though my job was to deliver "service", I was only thinking about survival. I wanted to know how to please the boss, control the company, and make all the money I could in the shortest amount of time.

My father started our air conditioning business in 1957. Working for him put extra pressure on me. I wanted his approval. I wanted to prove myself to him and to all the people who knew him. I worked longer and harder than anyone else. A typical day for me lasted 13 hours, but it wasn't unusual for me to stay 17 hours a day. I was a beginning manager and wasn't going to let anyone do more or know more than me. I was willing to pay any price to be number one.

I paid dearly, too. The company began to experience high turn-over. No one wanted to work for me and I didn't want them if they wouldn't please me. The stress on me was tremendous. Trying to control everything and everyone---and not doing a very good job of it. It was a nightmare! I was far too involved in the mess to clearly see what was happening.

One morning I got in my car, started it, backed up, and forgot to open the garage door. I smashed into it, of course. I got a hammer, beat the door until it opened, yelled at my wife, and drove off.

Two days later I got in the car, started it, backed up, and forgot to open the garage door again.

That's when I began to wake up.

I began to realize that maybe, just maybe, I was doing something wrong. I began to feel I was missing something. I began to question what I was doing as well as what I could be doing differently.

Gradually I changed. And so did the business. The company became more interested in its customers as we learned to think about taking care of people. I was still hooked into profit and loss, but at least I was becoming less "me" oriented. I recognized the need to care a little more about my employees and customers.

I took courses in personal development. I studied positive thinking, personalysis, Zig Zigler, the "One

Minute" everything, and other self-help material. I became familiar with the concept of "belief without evidence" and started thinking of my company in different terms. I started imagining a company where everyone worked together as a loving family dedicated to a common cause. Slowly, over time, I started to see that vision become a reality.

I knew I wanted to help people by offering them the service they wanted. But there was still a sense of righteousness involved. I wanted people to call *me*. I wanted my neighbors and family and friends to know I--- Ron McCann---was available to help them. I wanted to be their hero. I obviously wasn't totally self-less about this new ideal. My ego was still very much there.

In early 1988 I took Werner Erhard's two-weekend seminar, "The Forum." Through it I realized I actually couldn't control people or events. I understood that I could *share* my story with people without selling them on it. I realized that I had been trying to convince people that they needed me and my services. I began to see that what I could offer people was a gift, one which they could accept or reject as they so desired.

The Forum helped me understand that I had spent an awful lot of time and energy trying to please my father. I had been busy collecting evidence (more titles, more companies, more awards, etc), trying to prove I was as good as him. What I learned was that I could accept him for who he is. I learned to just be me. I began to feel deeply empowered, as if chains had been unlocked and I was suddenly free.

My growth didn't stop after The Forum. If anything, it accelerated. I began to look at all the possibilities in my life, all the ways I could serve and be served. I became more involved in church, civic and community activities. I became more interested in the lives of my family, friends and employees. And then, around Easter of 1988, I had a vision that altered my life.

I was in church, listening to the minister while contemplating the scene of the Last Supper and thinking about the experience of that Upper Room. As my mind explored the image, I saw that Jesus wanted to serve his disciples by washing their feet. I saw that the disciples didn't want that service because they (like me) wanted to please the boss. They wanted the Lord to look good. Washing feet seemed like a lowly thing for a savior to do.

Somehow I saw the whole picture. Jesus came here to serve and to be served. He was telling us that we, too, are here to serve and be served. Jesus *wanted* to wash his disciple's feet. Jesus *wanted* to serve. Because of their insecurity, the disciples declined.

It was an insight I'll never forget. I realized that my job is to serve people in whatever ways I find possible. *And* my job is to allow myself to *be* served whenever that opportunity arises.

I feel this is *your* mission as well. We are here to serve one another. Nothing more. Nothing less.

From that moment on I began to experience what I call "the joy of service." It is a feeling I often find hard to describe. The joy of service is a combination of conflicting emotions---like pride and humility---that arise whenever you unselfishly serve or receive service. That feeling is one you can't buy or manufacture. It's a rush of vibrating happiness that comes from within whenever you truly serve someone.

Now you know why I serve.

FOR MONEY OR LOVE?

Service isn't about making money. It's not the "profit hog" you're told it is. Service is doing something you love because you love it, and getting paid for what you do because you've done it exceptionally well.

I'm told that Walt Disney said he didn't make movies for money, he made money so he could continue making movies. Walt was right.

A business friend of mine sells bottled water. He's told me many times that he wants a profit so he can continue selling water. He doesn't want money for money's sake. He wants the profit so he can continue serving his community. He is dedicated to bringing quality water to his customers. In fact, my friend is more dedicated to delivering excellent water than his customers are to getting it. His clients sometimes see him as someone trying to make a sale. In reality, his desire is to give them the highest quality water imaginable. Isn't it interesting how we resist being served?

I've found that people who serve do so from an internal desire to give. In the book *Honest Business*, authors Michael Phillips and Salli Rasberry write, "Most of us who find service to be so important do so from a very deep inner sense."

The motivator isn't money. It's wanting to make a difference in the world through what you do. When you give service, when you work to serve your customers, you feel that joy of service. It's the joy that keeps you serving. It's that shivering, wonderful inner feeling that keeps you coming back for more.

You don't have to be in a "service business" to deliver service. Whatever you do, you are in some way, shape, or form, giving service. And that service touches the lives of people everywhere.

Let me give you four brief examples of what I mean.

* Andy Murphy is a newspaper salesman in Houston. He stands on a street corner seven days a week and sells papers to traveling motorists. He's been doing this for three years. "I enjoy doing what I do," he says. Andy has an inner peace, a serenity that touches the thousands of people he sees each week. And he sells 200 papers a day.

Andy is dedicated to delivering service.

* In a recent Houston article, Ellen Collier wrote about waiters. She said, "I doubt waiters realize their social power. They can add sparkle to any occasion and make or break a budding romance."

If only waiters knew how important service is!

* Barry Neil Kaufman serves parents by helping them heal children of autism and other "incurable" challenges. Why does he, his wife, and their staff devote their lives (7 days a week, 12 hours a day) to helping people? "Because I am happy doing this," Kaufman says.

Barry serves for the joy of serving.

* Gene Pavlovich has been sacking groceries part-time for thirteen years. He is 78 years old. Recently a Houston television station did a story on him because he is so popular with all the customers. Why does Gene serve people?

"I truly love my customers," Gene said. "It really makes me proud that at age 78 I have been accepted to continue serving my friends."

As you will learn in this book, we all serve. We have to. We live in a dependant world. You can't look out for "number one" because *there is no number one*! The world is a team. My mission is to awaken the world to the fact that each of us is here to serve and be served.

I serve people because it feels good for me to do that. I invite you to begin feeling the same experience.

How do you begin?

Just turn the page.

SERVICE TOOL #1

Serve for the *joy* of serving!

Chapter Two

WHAT IS SERVICE?

or,

What Do Hamburgers and Steel Have In Common?

*"The only two things people buy
are good feelings and solutions to
problems."*

--Michael LeBoeuf

Recently I saw a special on television about service in America. The reporters were glorifying McDonald's. They said the Golden Arches were providing a service millions of people needed, wanted and appreciated. The program went on to describe a new gas station billed as "Auto Gas." They called it "a great new service" because it wouldn't have any attendants. You pay with a credit card and everything would be computerized or automated.

Is McDonald's providing a service to you? Is a gas station without attendants a service? Is a miniature supermarket on a corner (called "Stop & Go") a service?

I say to you they are *not* services. What McDonald's, Auto-Gas and Stop & Go offer is convenience.

You go to McDonald's or any other fast food place because you want a hamburger *and* you want it quick. McDonald's is excellent at convenient hamburgers. That is what they distribute. A few decades ago it was profitable to produce and distribute steel. Now it is wiser to make and transport hamburgers. You drive up to a box, tell it you want a burger with or without cheese, and you drive around the corner, pay for it, and pick it up. The scenario is pretty much the same (and so are the burgers) no matter what fast food name you visit. They are masters at delivering convenient food.

That's not service.

You drive up to "Auto-Gas" and insert your credit card into a machine. You tell it what kind of gas you want. You put the fuel in yourself. Then you take your card out of the machine, put the cap back on your gas tank, and drive away.

That's not service.

You want something to drink---right on the corner (they are put there for a reason) is a "convenient" store. You go in, quickly grab what you need, pay for it, and leave.

That's not service either.

It is important that you and I begin on the same level of understanding. I don't feel convenience stores (whether you call them fast food places, grocery stops, or computerized gas stations) offer service. What those places offer is a quick-fix remedy to your current problem. Hungry? Grab a burger! Out of gas? Stop here! Need a loaf of bread? Look on the corner!

You probably realize there are restaurants known throughout your city for their hamburgers. You go in---a real live person greets you and seats you in a comfortable chair or booth. They give you a menu, bring you water, ask you how you are. You can order your burger cooked in a variety of gourmet ways. You can have coffee, sit and chat, relax, maybe even listen to live music.

That is a restaurant that provides a service.

Can you imagine a gas station where you drive in and the attendant comes to you, smiles, and asks how you are? He (or she) takes care of your car, washes your windows, checks your oil and transmission, puts air in your tires, and asks if you need anything else. Maybe this attendant notices your inspection sticker is out of date. He suggests you bring it around tomorrow for a new one. And before you leave he asks if you would like your car washed.

That is a gas station that provides a service.

Have you ever gone into a grocery store where everyone talks to you? Maybe they even know you and ask about your spouse. When you're curious about some exotic fruit, you ask about it. They stop whatever they are doing and tell you the history of the kiwi fruit. When you can't find something, you ask and they take you right to the product. When you check-out they ask if you need anything else. They offer to carry your bags to the car *or* they offer to deliver your groceries to your home!

That is a supermarket that provides a service.

Sure, you can order a pizza from a well-known fast food pizza maker and you'll have the food in twenty minutes. They'll deliver it right to your door. But is that service? They are offering you a convenience, but not service.

There are pizza places in your city where they make the finest pizza in the world. Places where you can go and be seated and have expresso coffee while you wait. Places that will bring you bread sticks, give you cloth napkins, and treat you like a king or queen.

Which do you want? Which one is more inviting?

The television show I saw made it sound like America had accomplished a lot by having such great "service." I take issue with that. I think America can brag about its great product delivery system, but specializing in fast burgers and pizza and auto gas is a sign of a nation in a rush because it's afraid to have relationships. It is a sign that we are alienating ourselves from one another.

RELATIONSHIPS THROUGH SERVICE

If you don't like the word service or serve, it's probably because the words have assumed a very negative connotation. Both come from the Latin word *servus*, which means "slave."

You can let go of that thought right now. People who serve are not slaves. Slaves are forced to do what people tell them. People who serve *choose* to serve.

When you begin to provide service because you choose to, out of joy, everything transforms. You no longer look at customers as people with money....suddenly they are people who need something. Suddenly their complaints are seen as requests. Suddenly you are a friend who can help them. You create a relationship when you serve them and, through that service experience, they serve you. A lot of creativity is required to begin, establish, and maintain that type of relationship. That is where the joy of serving comes into play. (Here's a thought for you to consider---maybe relationships are active only *while* we are serving one another.)

There is nothing wrong with fast hamburgers, pizza or gas. There *certainly* is a need for them. But we need to realize they are distribution channels for convenient delivery and *not* true service. An auto-teller is convenient. Going into a bank and requesting a transaction from a live person is a service---there's a major difference. In fast distribution any chance for a relationship has been eliminated, while true service depends on and thrives on relationships.

THE KEY

Relationships are the key to success, profit, and happiness as a server in business. Sometimes we decide not to offer service because we fear we might lose a relationship. I've heard people say "Don't work on your neighbor's air conditioner" or "Don't sell a car to a friend." There is risk in offering service. And maybe the risk is where the joy of service is felt. My suggestion here is for you to think of service as a gift. Offer your service without expectations and you will build new relationships while strengthening the ones you already have.

If you work for McDonald's, you can offer better service within that structure. If you own a gas station or a pizza parlor (or are thinking about it), this book will present new ways to make whatever you do more "service oriented and customer-driven."

If you think service (as I describe it) will cost too much, ask yourself a question: What does it cost you *not* to have service? People will go out of their way to sit in a restaurant that truly serves them. If you are a real server, location doesn't matter, but if your service is so-so, your location had better be "convenient."

If you think people want fast food over home-cooked meals, ask this question: Where do families go on Mother's Day or on Easter? Do you recall the aroma of McDonald's grill or your grandmother's kitchen?

You see, McDonald's may have good food. They may very well make a hamburger better than your

Grandmother. But we don't build relationships under the Golden Arches. (However, our children might!)

We have memories of Grandma's house. We recall friends, family and shared experiences. You don't always go to Grandma's for the food. You go there for the service, the feelings, the relationships. The talk before the meal, the conversation during the meal, and the relaxation after the meal is what makes Grandma's house special.

For just a moment, imagine going to Grandma's *only* for the food. You show up when the turkey is placed on the table and you leave right after you swallow the last bite. What do you think you missed? Do you think you enjoyed the dinner as much as the folks who came early and stayed late?

SERVICE TOOL #2

Don't substitute convenience for service.

Chapter Three

RECOGNIZING THE NEED FOR SERVICE

or,

Complaining as a Call For Service

*"Where I come from, service is
considered the greatest gift."*
--Valerie Andrew

Scene One: I'm in a meeting with my managers
and supervisors. I'm the President and they're
complaining about everything under the sun. I am feeling
threatened. I'm the boss and they shouldn't talk to me
like this! If they don't like it here they can leave! My
face is getting red. I'm getting angry. One manager pops
off and says, "You never listen to us!" I quickly respond,
"I'm listening *now*!" The situation is tense. I don't like
what I'm feeling. I don't like what I'm hearing. I call for
a ten-minute break to cool everyone off. Especially me.

I'm having a conversation with Stan Tyler, a
consultant friend of mine. He asks, "Ron, how are you

doing?" I tell him the truth. I feel angry. Hurt. Out of control. Ready to fire everybody for their blasted complaining. My friend just listens to me for a moment. In the pause I feel as though something historic is about to happen. Finally Stan quietly says, "Ron, a complaint is nothing but a disguised plea for help."

A complaint is a plea for help?

Scene Two: I'm lost. I'm in Albuquerque, New Mexico for the 17th annual International Balloon Fest and a computer programming conference. I'm looking for an evening gathering of computer resellers. I've been driving around a three-square mile area for over an hour, a car load of people with me and another car load behind me, following me, thinking I know where I'm going. I'm mad at the hotel manager for giving me lousy directions. I'm angry at the clerk at the corner store for drawing a vague map. And I'm furious at everybody responsible for the event for having it at such a hidden location.

At a red light I spot a police officer going the other way. I beep my horn and wave him over to me. When he pulls up I let him have it. I dump all my emotion-laden complaints on him. I tell him this city is ridiculous. The people are crazy and the streets are a maze. It never occurred to me that the man might arrest me for harassing him. But he just stood there and listened to me foam at the mouth. After a few minutes the officer calmly asks, "Where are you trying to go?" I tell him and he says, "Follow me. I'll take you right to it." He leads me to the party and shines a light on the entrance. I never would have found the place without his help, even though I was often not more than fifty feet from it during my search.

The policeman drove off. He didn't wait for a thank-you, or an acknowledgment. He didn't need his ego built-up. But because of his act of service I, and my two car loads of people, were able to have a wonderful time. We made a lot of friends, created business contacts, and shared information.

All because one man---a person committed to service excellence---heard my angry complaints as a call for help.

YOUR TURN

Now create your own scene. Recall the last time you complained to somebody. Maybe your office was too cold and you complained. Maybe you complained about being overworked. Maybe you complained about people complaining. It doesn't matter. Just think back to a time when *you* formed a complaint.

Why were you complaining? What was the message in your complaint? What were you *really* trying to say?

If your office was too cold, weren't you wanting to get heat? If you felt overworked, weren't you wanting to let someone know you needed help? And if you complained about people complaining too much, weren't you trying to say you cared and that the complaints were getting to you?

Now create one final scene: Think of the last time someone complained *to* you. What did he or she say? Were they angry? Maybe crying? How did you feel? Did you want to fix the problem or get rid of the complainer? Did you hear the message in the complaint? Did you realize the complaint was a call for help or did you get caught up in the emotion of the complaint? What did you do?

Whatever happened is okay. Use this exercise as a way to become aware of how you handle complaints and complainers.

THE TRUTH ABOUT COMPLAINTS

Carve these words on the top of your desk:
Every complaint is a request for service.
This is important enough to repeat:
Every complaint is a request for service!
Think about it.

Even the woman who walked up to your counter yesterday and yelled at you about getting poor service was really requesting more service. "You sent a plumber out here last week and my sink still leaks!" sounds like a complaint, doesn't it? It *is* a complaint. But inside that complaint is a request for service. The caller wants the sink fixed. Do you hear the complaint or the request? Are you caught in the emotion or do you clearly hear the call for help?

"I always have to wait for Becky to get off the terminal!" sure sounds like a complaint. But inside those words is a plea. The complainer wants to work on a terminal and can't. Do you react to the complaint or do you respond to the request for help?

"Management never listens to me!" is a complaint. And if you hear it as a complaint (as I did in the first scene of this chapter) you will get emotional. You won't address the real issue. The message in the words is a plea for help. The speaker is saying he or she doesn't feel heard. Do you think it is wiser to react to the complaint or to speak to the real issue?

Let me warn you about something that is crucially important. I know you might disagree with me about complaints. You might think complainers are ungrateful clods who ought to be dropped from the payroll. You might think complaints are unnecessary, pointless and often a waste of time. They're not.

At Herman Miller, Inc., Chairman Max DePree welcomed an employee who showed up in a sour mood. She snapped at him, "Don't you know two managers were just fired?!" Not only did he look into her complaint, he agreed that an injustice had been committed. And he rectified it. DePree said, "I consider it an enormous honor that I was approached with some expectation of fair play."

If you don't listen to complaints, if you don't invite complaints, you will cut your own throat! People complain because they want something. If they don't get what they want, they resign. They may not resign from the company, but they resign from life. They become the walking-dead on the job (and certainly not the "Grateful Dead"). Apathy will set in and the result will be unproductive co-workers and managers.

Can you afford that?

I know I can't.

I invite complaints in all my companies. There have been many occasions when employees have complained and even threatened to quit. But I have trained myself to hear the message in the complaint. I speak to the request, not the emotion. The result is clarity and power. The employee learns that I care, and we work together to solve whatever problem is at hand.

Teach yourself to understand that complaints are whispering screams for help. Learn to listen for the need inside the complaint.

WHY DO WE COMPLAIN?

You might very well be asking yourself, "If a complaint is a request for help, why don't people just request the help and quit complaining?"

Complaining is how we communicate. It's often the only way we know how to get what we want. Complaining is safe. When we ask for help with a request, the request can be answered with a yes or no. But a complaint isn't a question. It can't be rejected. It can only be heard or ignored.

Here's an example: A co-worker looks at you and says, "I can't possibly do all this work today!"

That's a complaint. You can ignore it if you want because it doesn't ask you to do anything. Not directly, anyway.

What if the same co-worker had looked at you and said, "Will you help me with all this work?"

Now you have a request to deal with. You can answer it with a yes or no. Which means the co-worker is put in a very vulnerable position. You might reject her. She knows it.

Can you see why complaints are a better strategy for most of us? A request can be denied and we feel hurt or rejected. A complaint is an emotional statement that doesn't ask you to do anything.

Complaints are also entertaining. Have you ever complained about something---anything---in a way designed to create laughter or tears? Haven't you eaten an apple at lunch and told everyone at your table about the ridiculous time you had with so-and-so? Did everyone laugh about it or maybe groan in frustration with you? Complaints are stories. They entertain us. They enroll us in a drama. The problem is that this type of communication doesn't help us. It doesn't forward our careers or our lives. We get caught up in the complaint and forget about the request *in* the complaint.

You can't expect people to communicate with requests. That is too uncomfortable for most of us. But you can invite people to complain. As odd as it may sound, you *have* to invite complaints. If you don't, your co-workers will die---from the inside out. Literally. And fast.

Fear of rejection turns a request into a complaint. If nobody hears the *request* in the complaint, people resign. No complaints. No action.

HOW TO STAY CLEAR

I'm not talking about how to stay clear of complaints. You should know by now that I think complaints are opportunities for personal growth. This section is about how to stay clear *in yourself* to hear complaints.

You probably don't like complaints. Most people don't. We take complaints personally. We get emotionally involved in complaints. We try to prove the complainer wrong. Or right. We do everything but truly listen.

If you rearrange the letters L-I-S-T-E-N in the right order you get the word S-I-L-E-N-T. Can you remain silent in yourself while hearing a complaint? Can you hear the other person without listening to your internal mental chatter? It is a special skill. But it is one you can learn. What it takes is self-awareness and *practice*.

Not very long ago one of our employees had a break-down and screamed that she wanted to quit; that she wasn't being treated fairly. Her immediate supervisor wanted to play the role of Florence Nightingale and fix the problem. Her manager, however, wanted to let the employee go. "If she's that unhappy," the manager said, "let her work someplace else!"

They all came to see me. I asked the employee what was wrong. I listened to her. She was very emotional. But I didn't get caught up in her emotion. I listened for her requests. She wanted to be treated fairly. What did she mean? She thought some parts of her job were stupid. Which parts? What would she rather be doing? She and I explored all the issues together. I stayed calm. I stayed focused. I knew her complaints were calls for help. I wanted to find out how I could help her. I wanted to hear lots of complaints.

The situation ended with her decision to stay on the job. We gave her some of the work she requested. She later told us that she never realized how much we cared about her. Most likely, for possibly the first time in her career, someone heard her plea for help and responded. Someone listened.

What she wanted was help. Not nursed, fixed, or fired. Help!

Her supervisor and manager have since learned to use listening as a valuable tool. They now find many opportunities to help people move from complaints to action.

How do you respond to complaints? Understanding what you *already* do is the first step toward change. Think about the way you feel when someone confronts you with a complaint. You can't change their feelings, but you can change yours. Imagine what it might be like to listen to a person with an open, calm mind and heart. What would it be like to look at a complainer as a person needing some form of service?

You may not change your attitude toward complaints overnight. But you can begin the transition right now. As many times as possible, whenever the need arises, remind yourself that a complaint is a request for help. And learn to listen for the request.

Hear customers' complaints as your opportunity to help. Hear co-workers' complaints as their desire to improve some existing condition.

Here's an illustration that may clarify the steps in this positive progression:

HEAR THE REQUEST

CONSIDER SOLUTIONS

MAKE A PROMISE

TAKE ACTION

First, hear the request in the complaint. Second, consider the possibilities. Third, make a promise to do something that responds to the request. Fourth, take action consistent with your promise.

Let me give you a simple example: You hear the complaint "I hate working from 8 to 5!" as a request for different hours. You consider that possibility. Can you let the employee work from 9 to 6? Is that possible? You then commit to the new time arrangement, or to investigating if it is possible, or you say "No, we can't do that. But what else is possible in this situation?" You then take some form of action based on your commitment.

What I do with people is listen for possibilities. So if someone feels they have a complaint, I listen. I know they have a request of some sort. And that request may lead to greater productivity, better relationships, or something so great I can't even imagine. But first I have to listen for the possibilities. If I think I know all the answers, all I ever get is what I have always gotten. But if I listen with an open mind, then the world opens and *anything is possible*.

WHAT PEOPLE WANT

I listen because people with complaints want to be helped. And if I want to serve people, I have to listen.

It may not be easy, but it *is* simple.

SERVICE TOOL #3

Remember: Inside every complaint is a request for service.

Chapter Four

JUDGING SERVICE

or

How to Become Irresistible

"The Smith and Hawken policy book says this: It has to feel right. Feeling right counts for everything because when the product and the money are exchanged, a feeling, sweet or sour, is what we're left with."

--Paul Hawken

When do you begin to judge a person? Do you wait until you know him or her better? Do you reserve all judgment for two or three weeks and *then* decide whether you like that person or not? Or do you arrive at some conclusions as soon as you meet the person?

There was a book written a while back called *The First Three Minutes*. The thought behind it was that we make judgments about people within three minutes of

31

meeting them. And people judge you and me that quickly too. First impressions may not be explainable or definable, but they are felt. And they are real. Once a judgment is made, it is incredibly difficult to change. Like it or not, we do judge a book by its cover!

When do you judge a company? Do you wait until you get service? Do you wait until after you've eaten your meal to decide if you like the restaurant? At what point do you say "I like this company" or "I'll never do business with those people again!"?

We judge companies as quickly as we judge people. I hope you hear this point and remember it. It is essential to your well-being as a service business and as a server in business. You are judged as soon as a person makes contact with you in *any* way. You don't have to meet a person to be judged by them. Somebody will look at your work and decide if they like you. A person will take a look at your home or office and decide if they want to be your friend or do business with you. You are judged on more than your words and actions. You are judged on everything that relates to you in any way.

Pretty scary thought, isn't it?

Botch one job and you may never be forgiven. Come to work in shabby clothes, with a hangover, and you may be judged for life. Have a poor ad in the Yellow Pages and people will decide you aren't professional. A faulty seat on an airplane might be interpreted as bad engine maintenance.

Realize that what you do touches many people in many ways. People make judgment-calls about you before they ever meet you. They see your work and judge you. They see your office and judge you. They see your dress and judge you. They see your friends and judge you.

Don't become paranoid. Be aware of how you can become irresistible in your business as well as personal life. The first step is to realize you are judged all the time---whether you are present or not. The most crucial contact of all is the *first* one, whether it is a telephone conversation or at the front door, an advertisement, or a referral. Your customer forms an opinion of you instantly.

THE SECRET TO BEING IRRESISTIBLE

How do you become irresistible?

Manage your Moments of Truth. Karl Albrecht, author of *Service America!*, says that a Moment of Truth is any episode in which a customer comes in contact with any aspect of an organization and gets an impression of the quality of its service.

Jan Carlzon, President of Scandinavian Airlines, understood that customers judge his business on more than the flight. When they call up the airline they judge the clerk who answers the phone. When they drive to the airport they judge the parking lot. When they enter the airport terminal they judge your sign, location and appearance. When they check-in they judge the clerks and the service. Carlzon says a Moment of Truth is every single moment a customer experiences from the moment they decide they have a need for service.

Carlzon said there are over 50,000 Moments of Truth a day!

And you have to have a quality control finger on every one of those Moments of Truth. Why? Because you don't know which moment a potential customer will judge.

Imagine this: You are interviewing people to hire a new employee. You have a stack of resumes on your desk. Some of them are handwritten (I've seen some that way). Some resumes are typeset. Some are ten pages long. Most are one or two pages. Which do you read first? Do you go to the ones that look attractive and professional? Do you make judgments about the applicants based only on the papers before you? You may even trash the resumes that are handwritten---even when there is a possibility that the applicant may be perfect for the job!

The person who sent you the hand written resume did not know a resume was a Moment of Truth.

And now you are interviewing applicants for the job. One person (we'll say it's a woman but of course, it could be either) walks in rather quickly and complains about having to fill out the job application when she already sent a resume. This makes you feel uncomfortable. She is a little too arrogant, too talkative, too this and that. Even if her credentials are flawless, you tell her "Don't call us, we'll call you!"

Another person enters your office. Nicely dressed, polite, a little nervous but understandably so under the situation. His or her resume isn't as impressive as the first, but you like this person's friendliness and style. What do you say to this person? Do you tell him (or her) to meet the manager for a second interview?

Now a third person comes in for an interview. You have been anxious to meet this one. His resume looks outstanding. His education and experience are exactly what you need. You almost want to hire him before you meet him. But then you *see him*. He looks like he has been working in the yard all day. He has a monotone voice and doesn't look you in the eye. Do you hire him anyway? Not if the position has contact with the public!

Here's a sobering thought: What impression are *you* making on these job applicants? Those people sitting across from you, desperate for a job, are looking at you and judging your entire company. What do they think if they see twenty other resumes on your desk? How do they feel about your business when you keep them waiting thirty minutes in the lobby?

My point is that we make judgments every step of the way---*before* we ever meet. Your resume is judged before you get an interview. Your business is judged before you ever see a customer.

To succeed in business, to be able to serve the customer, you have to manage every Moment of Truth.

How do you do that? How do you control *every single* Moment of Truth? You can't control them all, so you better control all the Moments you can get your hands on!!!

You need to do a little role playing. Pretend you are the customer choosing a business offering your services. In other words, if you are a lawyer, how do people find you? In the yellow pages? Okay. What kind of ad do you have? You will be judged on it. Do people hear of you from other lawyers? Okay. What kind of reputation do you have? Word-of-mouth is the strongest advertising in existence. If you do not get good recommendations, why not? Do people hear of you from your past cases? What will they hear? If your cases get publicity, you had better handle your cases with wisdom.

Are you a salesperson? Your product has a reputation as well as you. When people hear about your product, what do they think? When people contact you, what impressions do you make? Are you open and friendly or closed and pushy?

If you are a manager, you will be judged on the performance of your staff. So how is your staff doing? Do they realize that what they do---from how they enter the door to how they perform their jobs---is a Moment of Truth for you, for them, and for the company?

ARE YOU INVITING?

In 1981 Houston's Hobby Airport was undergoing expansion. Flights were not hindered, but getting in and out of Hobby by *car* was a migraine headache!

Construction was going on everywhere. Where do you park to pick up arrivals? Where is long-term parking? Where do you return a rental car?

The rental companies and the airlines could have invested in a few signs. They could have taken advantage of a golden opportunity to control their long-term image. Today, years after the construction has been completed and all the problems solved, people who haven't seen the new facility still think of Hobby Airport in a negative way. Those people may *never* go back!

If you want to serve and be served, you have to manage your Moments of Truth.

Why? It should be obvious. Would you want an accountant with a bad reputation? Neither would I. So that accountant must repair his image before he can serve us.

You won't have the opportunity to serve *anyone* if your Moments of Truth are not managed. People will pass you by.

Would you rather eat in a clean restaurant or a dirty one? Even if the dirty restaurant *wants* to serve, they will get little or no business. Why? Because all you know about the business is from the sign out front. If the sign looks like it belongs in front of a greasy spoon, we assume the restaurant is just that and we may never drive in.

If you call for a cab and two show up, do you get in the shiny one or the dirty one? (Back up a step. When you looked in the phone book for a cab service, which ad did you choose? Did you judge the taxi before you ever saw it, based on the image of their advertisement?)

Managing your Moments of Truth is how you invite service. Whether you are submitting a resume, working for a client, or opening a business, learn to manage your image by managing your Moments of Truth.

It's really not an awesome task. If you are committed to service, if you truly want to serve the world, then you have to know that people only come to you if they are attracted to you. They only come when you *invite* them.

Think like someone who would use your service. Trace their steps. Follow the path that leads to your door. Then be sure every single step on that trail is an invitation to excellent service.

Some banks and retailers hire people to test the service they deliver. They employ a person to walk through the bank and test their Moments of Truth. The "paid shopper" reports to the bank about the experience. The bank then shares the results with the front line. It's an excellent program that helps the banks control the way they look to their customers.

People will come to you for your service *if* you make the way easy, attractive and inviting.

A Moment of Truth exists whenever a potential client or customer has a choice. They can choose your service, or the service of someone else. They will *always* decide in your favor if you have managed your Moments of Truth.

Don't overlook the little things. How you answer the phone when the spouse of a co-worker calls is just as important as how you answer it when a customer calls. Do you realize that spouses make judgments about you and your work, too? Their conversations at home about how they were treated can affect the image you present to customers, even your own image of the company. Be aware that how the phone is answered when *anyone* calls is an important Moment of Truth.

Managing all your Moments of Truth is how you invite service. It is how you become irresistible.

SERVICE TOOL #4

Remember: Manage your Moments of Truth
and you will become irresistible.

Chapter Five

WHO DO YOU SERVE?

or,

The Chain of Command vs. The Pyramid

*"If you're not serving the customers,
you'd better be serving someone who
is."*

--Karl Albrecht

Who do you serve?

There is a lot of talk these days about becoming "customer-driven." But do you know who your customers *really* are?

The way to answer the question "Who do I serve?" is to ask yourself a different one: "Who benefits from my work?"

You may be surprised to discover who your customers are. Often you aren't working for the public or for an employer. You may be working for another staff member. Your boss may even be working for *you*. There is a significant difference between who you *report to* and who you *work for*.

THE PYRAMID

At McCannics Home Services we use an inverted pyramid to describe our organization. It helps us see who we serve.

Take a look at this customer-driven organizational chart. You will note that the President (me) is at the bottom of the chart, not the top. The people the President serves are the managers, not the public. My "customers" are my managers!

McCannics' managers do not serve me. They serve the people above *them* on the chart. If a manager wants to know how well he is doing, he doesn't ask me. He asks the staff that reports to him. They benefit from the manager's work and only they know if he is doing his job. The manager works for his staff.

If you are the Payroll Clerk, you serve the people who receive payroll checks. Your work goes directly to the employees. As the Payroll Clerk, your "customers" are the employees.

You *never, ever* do the payroll for your manager! You do the payroll for your fellow employees. The better you do it, the less your boss has to get involved. Your boss isn't responsible for the payroll. You are. Your boss is really a troubleshooter and back-up for you. Your boss is responsible for seeing that you have what you need to perform your job---and *your* job is to get the payroll to your customers.

Note that when I (as a manager) sign those checks I am serving you (the payroll clerk) not the employees. Though the employees ultimately benefit from my doing my work (just as I benefit from them doing theirs) when I sign the checks, I am doing it to serve the Payroll Clerk. If I don't sign those checks the Payroll Clerk (you, if that's your position) is the first to know and the first to complain.

You might argue that you *must* be serving your boss because that's who you call when you're going to be late for work. But who you report to is often *different* from who you serve. You *report* to your boss. He does not necessarily receive your work so you don't necessarily work *for* him. A repair technician will call his immediate supervisor if he is ill. The technician is simply passing along needed information in the "chain of command." The technician's "customer" is the public because the public directly benefits from his work.

Who directly benefits from your work? *That* person is your customer.

If each person you work with knows who they serve, then the operation will run more smoothly. Know who *your* customer is and serve that person (or persons). They are the ones you must satisfy to have a truly service-oriented, customer-driven business.

THE CHAIN OF COMMAND

Employees often try to please the boss, not the people they serve. Some managers worry so much about their impression on the boss, they forget to sign the checks or review a report to serve the accountant. This self-centered approach creates a breakdown in the customer-driven organization. Everyone is out to please the boss while the *true customer* is left with nothing.

You have seen how that system works, haven't you? How many times have you called for service, met with the representative or repairman and then not gotten the service you expected? What happens when you ask the person to repair something he was not told to fix? He often says, "I'll have to check with my boss." You see, service people are often told to do the job and nothing more. They have to check back with the boss (the commander) if you ask them to do something extra.

I say that isn't service. I say that is pleasing the boss---and the boss isn't always the customer!

We were taught by our forefathers in business to please our boss or manager or employer. We all were. That is an old school of thought which sets up a "chain of command" organization to serve the boss. Where is the customer in the chain? The boss is in charge of the customer and everyone else does exactly what they are *told*. Most businesses based on the old chain of command system (and most businesses *use* the old system) have an organization chart that resembles a set of chains linked together. At the top of the chart is the "supreme commander," the boss.

Who serves the paying customer in the chain? In fact, the only people really working for the public are the people who communicate with the public, which in this case are the repair-technicians. Who do those technicians strive to please? Their *supervisors*, of course. These technicians can not focus on the customer's needs because they are trying so hard to please their supervisors. In fact, if you ask those technicians a question like "What or who are you working for?" they will tell you, "I'm working for my paycheck" or "I'm working for my boss!"

Who do their *bosses* want to please? Their own immediate supervisors. Who do the managers want to please? Whoever is above them in the chain of command, of course!

Unfortunately, in the "chain of command" structure, orders are given to subordinates with little regard to input from the front line. "You're paid to do as you're told, not to think." (Remember *that* one?)

Orders from the top often bind the performance of front line servers to rules and regulations that do not respond to the customer's needs. The "supreme commander" is buffered by middle management out to please him.

NORDSTROM

This department store chain based in Seattle is known for delivering extraordinary service to its customers. In my travels I came across a young lady employed by a competitive department store based in Texas. She was sent by her employer as a paid shopper to Nordstrom to discover the secret of their excellent customer satisfaction rate. She tried every trick in her shopper's notebook to create the possibility of dissatisfaction. She wore a dress one evening, tore it intentionally, and returned it. To her surprise (and to her employer's dismay) each Moment of Truth was managed impeccably. What she discovered as the secret of Nordstrom's success was their constantly practiced Nordstrom Rule. We should all live by the Nordstrom Rule documented in the Nordstrom employee handbook:

WELCOME TO
NORDSTROM
We're glad to have you with
our Company.
Our number one goal is to provide
outstanding customer service.
Set both your personal and
professional goals high.
We have great confidence in your
ability to achieve them.

Nordstrom Rules:

Rule #1: **Use your good
judgment in all situations.**
There will be no additional rules.

Please feel free to ask
your department manager,
store manager or division general
manager any question
at any time.

So often the "chain of command" employees expect supervisors to tell them what to do. How can supervisors make company decisions in favor of the customer when they don't really know the needs of the customer? I suggest every organization consider allowing the front-line servers a say in managing the customers. No one knows the customers or what they need better than the front-line people.

You should be able to see that the "chain-of-command" approach is arranged to carry out commands. It is a military command operation where the goal is to please the boss. It is *not* service-oriented or customer-driven.

Now take another look at the inverted pyramid. Who works for the paying customer? *Everyone*! This new chart shows that the customer is king and everyone, ultimately, has to work for the customer, making decisions based on what the customer wants.

Do you see the difference?

In the "chain-of-command" chart everyone is trying to please the boss and move up the ladder. In the pyramid chart everyone works for the paying customer and knows that each person they work for is, in a real way, a customer, too.

Understanding the differences in these charts is important. The "chain-of-command" or "please-the-boss" approach is the way most companies are run. "Pleasing the boss" is not in favor of the customer-driven organization. The pyramid "everyone-is-a-customer" approach means the entire organization works together to serve each other while serving the true boss and employer: the paying customer.

WHAT THE CHAIN OF COMMAND IS GOOD FOR

The chain of command has its uses. You can look at it as your "report-to" chart. If you want to know who to ask for help, or who to call when your car breaks down and you're going to be late for work, look at the chain of command. The chain of command display is your company's chain-of-command blueprint. It tells you who the bosses are.

By contrast, the pyramid is your "work-for" chart. If you want to know who your customers are, look at the pyramid. If you want to know who you serve, look at the pyramid. The inverted pyramid reveals your true customers (the people who benefit directly from your work).

If you are now catching the "joy of service" fever, you need to know who your *customers* are. The pyramid will tell you just that. You also need to know who your *boss* is, and that's where the "chain of command" comes in handy. After all, I'm *not* telling you to ignore your boss! You need to have the support of your boss to do your job, but most of all, you need to know who your *customers* are if you want to serve them.

In short, you need both charts. The "chain of command" identifies the boss to report your needs to.

The pyramid reveals who your customers are. Since your customer usually isn't your boss, you need both charts.

One more thing: Don't confuse the charts! Don't look at the chain of command to learn who your customers are and don't look at the pyramid to find your boss! The charts have different functions. Know what they are!

But remember: The world is better served by knowing who you work for rather than who you report to!

HOW TO HANDLE A COMMANDER

I know that you might be in a job where everyone in the company lives by the chain of command. You may be a secretary, a nurse, an accountant or a repair-technician. You understand that your customer is whoever you hand your work to and not necessarily your boss. Yet your boss wants you to please him (or her). Your boss demands that you do what the company wants and your boss seems, we'll say, close-minded. He thinks he is looking out for the company and you aren't. You may have heard him say, "Do what I say or leave!" Or maybe he has said, "My way or the highway!"

What do you do? How do you begin to serve your true customers while satisfying the commander?

The answer is simple. You set an example. You do whatever the boss requests *while* doing your best to serve the customer. You continue to report your activities to your boss but you work for your customers.

If you are a dispatcher, your customers are the people in the trucks needing exact information. Do that job to the best of your ability so your customers (the repair technicians) can do their jobs.

If you are a clerk in word-processing, your customers are the people you hand the finished documents to. Your boss doesn't need to know that you are courteous and punctual and that you did extra typing for the managers in marketing, but you can *report* that to him or her if you want. Do whatever needs to be done in the best way possible so your customers (the people who asked you to do the typing) can do their jobs.

Some people complain when they are asked to do something by someone they serve (someone other than their boss). These people want the commander to okay the request first. You *cannot* give extraordinary service if you maintain this approach. Your boss is there to schedule the time and supply you with the necessary resources to get the job done. Your boss is not there to pass judgment on your every move. (If you are a boss, you will want to read the next chapter. It's written specifically for you.)

When you try to please the boss, you don't always please your customers. The boss (if he or she is living by the chain-of-command) is looking out for the company, not the customer. And that is understandable. The chain of command has been around a long time. It is *not* wrong. It is simply an old approach to business. I am now offering you a new, more genuinely customer-oriented approach.

When you try to please your customers, you should as a direct result please your boss. When you work for and satisfy your true customers, you will be doing your job. Your boss may be uncomfortable with this at first. He or she will probably resist change. Most of us do. Don't feel too bad about this. I believe 95% of the managers out there still worship the chain-of-command. I also believe that your boss will change before your co-workers do. Your boss will recognize excellent service and will be quick to join you in the whole atmosphere that I simply call "the joy of service."

Don't fight your boss! He who holds the gold, makes the rules. Max DePree also said "Having a say does not mean having a vote."

Don't wait for your boss to direct you to be an excellent server. Don't wait for him to add this chapter to your company manual.

Look at it this way: If your children wanted to be more organized at home, would you want them to clear it with you first? Does your spouse have to ask permission to cook a wonderful meal before you will recognize it as a wonderful meal? Of course not. Everyone recognizes the results of excellent service (though we don't always acknowledge what we get). You don't have to ask permission to serve.

It all comes back to serving your customers. To do that, you need to know who *your* customers are. Who benefits from your work? Who do you hand your work to or do it for? Who directly uses the result of your work?

Answer those questions and you'll begin to understand who your customers *really* are.

SERVICE TOOL #5

Remember: Take care of your customers
and invite your boss to take care of you.

Chapter Six

HOW TO BE A WINNING COACH

or,

A Special Note for Managers Only

"Most of what we call management consists of making it difficult for people to get their work done."
                    --Peter Drucker

I am writing this book for the front-line servers in business. I am writing this for the people you call "employees." But I want you to know that *you*---the manager---are an employee and a server, too.

As I pointed out in the previous chapter, the people you serve are the people who directly benefit from your work. As a manager, you serve your staff of employees. *Your* customers are your staff. Your job is to see that your staff is provided the resources to satisfy the needs of their customer. In a sense, you are a coach in charge of your staff's well-being.

As Jan Carlzon told his managers (as reported in *At America's Service*), "You are not here to dictate to the front line. You are here to help them, to support them. And when they ask you for help, you have to listen to them, and not the other way around."

Most managers are uncomfortable with this idea. I deal with mid-management every day. What they want is to survive and they have learned to do this by playing the game of "pleasing the boss." You know the system. Always wear a gray suit, never openly disagree with the boss, always find out what the boss wants and give it to him, learn what he likes to hear and say it, and so on.

In the movie "Bull Durham" a veteran player takes a rookie aside and tells him exactly what to say in an interview. Every line is preprogrammed, non-controversial, and designed to keep the player safe. Now I notice every major league baseball player interviewed says these same lines!

Like the ballplayer, most managers make a career out of learning how to be safe. The best way for you or any manager to remain safe is always look good to your boss.

I'm here to tell you that the "pleasing-the-boss" approach doesn't serve *your* customers at all. It serves you, it may serve your boss, but it *does not* serve your staff! Again, your customers are the people in your department and not your boss. Your main responsibility as a manager is to take care of your staff. The *staff* does the work, not you!

Ideas are always easier to explain when we use specific examples. So let's say you are a manager in charge of the accounting department. You probably think you are responsible for the accuracy of every check and every book. You want to control your department so you can manage the results. You have a set of rules you feel ought to be followed.

In short, if you (like most managers) feel that *you* and *you alone* are responsible for the results of your department, that is the way most boss-pleasing managers think. Though that mindset has probably worked for you, I'd like to offer a more satisfying alternative.

I suggest that managers are in *no* way responsible for the results of their staff.

I suggest that your responsibility as a manager is for the well-being of the people who report to you. So, if you are the manager of the accounting department, you are responsible for the well-being of the staff in that department. You are there to take care of their needs.

And that's *all* you are responsible for!

When you manage your staff's well-being, everything else falls into place. You don't have to worry about anything *except* whether your players are well or not. You don't have to double-check every ledger or look over the shoulder of every employee. You don't have to set up a strict code of procedures and you don't have to act like a parent to your staff, ready to solve everyone's problems and be the hero.

All you have to do is manage the well-being of your staff.

That's it!
Let me explain.

THE TRUTH ABOUT MANAGING

You cannot manage an organization.

In the first place an organization isn't a reality. It doesn't live. Can you talk to a company? Can you shake hands with an organization? An organization is a collection of people working for a common cause. A successful manager has to learn how to manage individuals. Do that, and the *people* will run the organization.

How do you manage people?

How does a coach manage a football or basketball team? He looks out for the players. If a player is missing shots, that player is put in a position where he passes off or rebounds. If a player is unhappy and performing poorly, you find out what position he really wants and put him there. Or maybe you trade him because he'd be happier elsewhere (but you find out what *he* wants first).

You don't manage the team by a set of rules. You manage the team by what the individuals need to be well. Well-being means many things, but mostly happiness or satisfaction. If your individuals are happy, if they are in a state of well-being, they will do their job at an optimal level of performance. If your staff isn't happy, you will see it in their performance, and you will know you need to do something to help them regain wellness.

Take a simple example: You set the temperature in your department to 74 . Suddenly one person says he is cold and another says she is warm. You can't make a company-wide decision that says 74 degrees is the law because that won't work! What you can do is give the cold person a sweater and the warm one a fan. You manage their well-being. You satisfy their needs so they can do their work.

Here's a more sophisticated example: Someone wants to take off at 4:30 tomorrow. The rules say everyone works till 5:00. What do you do? If you manage by the rules, you'll deny the time off. But if you manage by the well-being of the individual, you'll try to work something out. Maybe that person can come in early and leave early that day. Maybe he can take a short lunch so he can leave sooner than usual. You consider the possibilities so your employee can remain in a state of well-being. (Of course, if the employee is consistently asking for time off, you might want to find out why. Certainly, something is wrong.)

If you focus on the well-being of your people, you will naturally manage everyone in a smooth, caring, productive way. This is an important point. Too many managers are so busy looking good to their own boss that they neglect the needs of their staff. Too many managers try to manage the work the staff does instead of allowing the staff to do their own work.

A manager who serves his staff is one who performs the function of a good coach---he doesn't play the game for the players, he simply sees that everyone has what they need to play. You don't have to do your staff's work. You only have to see that they have what they need so *they* can do it. To put it another way, you don't get paid for what you do, you get paid for what your staff does.

WELL-BEING RULES

Managing by well-being doesn't mean you have to abandon company rules.

McCannics Home Services has organizational rules. These rules were created with the employee's well-being in mind. One of our rules is: People are not allowed to take coffee to their desks and they *must* take breaks.

Seems weird, doesn't it? Why do you think we created that rule? How do you think it serves the employee?

In most companies people drink coffee right at their desk. That prevents relationships. If people take breaks at regular intervals, and if they have to drink coffee in the same break room, then they have a greater opportunity for relationships. People are in a state of well-being when they get regular breaks *and* when they have the opportunity to be with other people. This also creates a family atmosphere. So our rule serves the employee in a very direct way.

Here is another example of a company rule designed to serve the employee: To get paid for a holiday the employee must work either the day *before* or the day *after* the holiday. Why did we make this rule? How does it serve the employee?

Years ago nearly all our employees were choosing to take their vacation at the holidays. That meant that whoever worked the holiday had to run the entire ship. This skeleton crew obviously was not in a state of well-being---they were overworked.

Now, with our new rule, all employees are assured that no individual has to stay behind and run the show for everyone else. We keep an adequate number of employees at work at all times. No one gets overworked. Everyone remains in a state of wellness.

You don't have to surrender your rules. Just make sure your rules serve your employees and not some *company*. After all, your employees *are* your company. Serve your employees and you will be serving your company. Caring for people is an active job.

I can't tell you how to care for your staff, but if you do care for them, and help them stay well, they will do their jobs better than you could ever imagine.

"IT'S NOT MY JOB"

How can you begin serving your staff? One way is to begin to listen to them. I mean *really* listen. Actually ask for complaints---and then listen to those complaints in an attentive, caring way. Those complaints will be a clue to what your staff needs in order to be well.

The other thing you can do right now to serve your staff is to quit playing the role of fixer or know-it-all. As I mentioned earlier, too many managers like to solve problems *for* their staff. It builds up the manager's ego. When you solve problems for your staff, you take away their power. You actually do them a dis-service.

If you get a call from a client about a problem in your department, you have a choice: You can say, "Julie will handle it" and then let Julie handle it, or you can say, "I'll take care of it." In the former you put the power right where it belongs---with the person who does that job. If Julie needs any help, she can come to you. You see, if you do her work for her, you steal Julie's power by acting as a fixer.

I was taught never to say "It's not my job" to someone. I suggest that to be a successful manager you have to say something to that effect.

I know this is dangerous for you. The politics of management say play it safe. You've learned to please your boss and you've learned to be a prince or princess to your staff. I'm now suggesting you do something radically different. I'm encouraging you to truly serve your customers---your own staff. I'm inviting you to be a coach to your people.

Are you up to the challenge?

SERVICE TOOL #6

Managers are not responsible for the *work* people do, but for the *people* who do the work.

Chapter Seven

GOING BEYOND KNOWN SERVICE

or,

Look Outside the Nine Dots!

"Never put your personal convenience ahead of that of your customer."

--from the employee handbook of Whole Foods Market

Do you like to make phone calls to strangers and try to sell them magazines, refrigerators or your service? Most people hate it. Telemarketing is traditionally seen as an undesirable job. Most people in telephone sales probably began because they needed part-time work. Calling strangers and giving a boring sales pitch is thought to be tiring and frustrating. After a while everyone you talk to on the phone become similar. Prospects are no longer individuals with unique histories and needs. They are voices who either say "I'm interested in what you're selling," "No, I don't need that", or "Leave me alone!"

You probably never wanted to be in collections either. It is typically regarded as a fight-for-your-life position. You call innocent people on the phone and harass them until they pay you. Collectors are usually taught to be cold, mean, and single-minded. Customers who owe you money are seen as the enemy. They are criminals in the eyes of the collector. Your job as a collector is to be a type of bounty-hunter. You go after those criminals until they pay up, and if they don't come across, you stick the law on them. It's not a position where you make a lot of friends.

So, how do you create telemarketing and collections in such a way that they actually serve the customer?

LOOK OUTSIDE THE NINE DOTS!

The first thing you have to do is abandon your usual mode of problem-solving. If you look at those functions as you have always been taught to look at them (Who's right? Who's wrong? What's the bottom-line?), then you won't see any room for change or improvement. Look at them with fresh eyes, with a creative, open mind, and then you might come up with new possibilities.

Would you like to stretch your mind right now? Here's a simple experiment. Look at the nine dots and connect them with four straight lines. Don't retrace a line or let your pen leave the paper. Go ahead. Try it!

How did you do? Though you may have seen this test before, it's often very hard to figure out. Look on the next page for the solution.

You probably tried to solve this puzzle by creating lines within the dots. The solution lies *outside* the dots! That's where you have to look to solve any problem creatively. When you look inside the dots you use a standard, already known mindset. If you look *outside* the dots, if you start to entertain new possibilities you begin to think more creatively.

Now let's apply this "look outside the dots" approach to telemarketing and collections!

HOW TO COLLECT MONEY OWED YOU

What would your collections department look like if it were out to serve the customer?

During my twenty years of business experience I've noticed that the people who successfully collect money often become company presidents and owners. Why? I believe it is because efficient collectors create beneficial relationships with customers. A customer who can't pay is a customer with a problem. A creative bill collector, a person who wants to serve the customer, will find a way to help that customer out of his predicament. Customers don't forget helpful people. Customers very often remain so loyal that they inadvertently help the server become a company president, manager or owner.

If you are in collections, memorize this rule: Agreement gets you money. It is the secret to collecting whatever is owed to you.

Demand money and you get arguments. Lawyers demand money and what do they get? *Loads* of battles. Agreement, not argument, gets money. Seek agreement.

Now, what if you are on the phone with someone who owes you $350 and they tell you they can't pay? Obviously fighting with them will not work. Arguing, harassing, threatening or sending more bills won't work, either. If they don't have the money, squeezing them for it is unproductive.

What do you do?

Keep in mind the idea that you really want to serve this customer. If you want to serve him, would you torture him with relentless phone calls? *No!* If your goal is to serve, you will talk to the customer to find out how you can help. You will look outside the nine dots. Maybe he can't pay $350, but he can pay $50 and commit to monthly payments. If you stick to the bottom-line company rules, you will only look for $350. But if you treat the customer as a friend who has a problem, you will be creating a new and different way to serve.

Sandi, one of our managers in the collection department, once told me she gets results because she is firm and focused, yet friendly. Her calls to overdue customers are requests, not demands, for payment. She creates a relationship with the customer. That's where the joy of serving resides. If someone says "I can't pay" she responds with "How can I help you pay?" Sandi strives for agreement and is always there to serve the customer. She looks for creative solutions.

It takes imagination and guts to work in the collections department with an attitude of service. Maybe serving a customer means calling them every day until they pay. Some customers hesitate to commit to anything. You may have to serve them by reminding them that they owe you money. Get agreement from the customer to allow you to call them, but you don't have to threaten them! If you are here to serve, you don't talk to a customer with an overdue bill as if he or she were on the Ten Most-Wanted list!

Remind yourself: If I truly want to serve this customer, how will I treat him? What can I do to help him? What is possible in this situation that I haven't yet considered?

HOW TO MAKE PHONE SALES WORK

What would your telemarketing department look like if it, too, were truly there to serve the customer?

Most employees regard telemarketing as boring. Some companies are buying computers and machines that make sales calls. Isn't there a creative way to do phone sales while serving the customer?

Automated calling machines used to solicit business irritate customers. Why? Because machines are not creative, they don't listen.

We don't use telemarketers at McCannics Home Services. We created Customer Service Reps. We have people who understand that you have to get into relationships with customers in order to serve them. Our Customer Service Reps are people who make friends with the customer and genuinely want to serve them. They aren't trying to make a sale, they are trying to serve.

Again, just wanting to serve people will transform how you do all your business. If you are here to serve, you don't read a script to sell someone a product.

(Remember, if you truly want to serve and be successful at it, look outside the nine dots!)

A fellow businessman and a good friend of mine has created a method for selling that is unique. The first thing he does when he calls someone is ask "If you have a minute, I'd like to talk to you about a product that I think you might want to know about." He doesn't come on like gang busters and storm the client with a barrage of tricks. He is open and honest. He knows his call is an intrusion in that person's day. He treats people like people. He tries to serve them by being sincere. That is *very* different from the way you may have thought you were suppose to make a sales call!

If you routinely ask yourself the question, "Am I serving this person?", then you will always think of the person you are calling and not of yourself. You should never make a call unless you know your intention is to serve the person you are calling. People don't want to be sold, they want to be served!

The difference is in your attitude. If you make sales calls by reading a script, you'll fail. You will make a few sales but you'll have a lousy time. If you make calls with the idea that you are making friends and helping people, then your life---*and* the customer's---will be enriched. You will increase sales too! Think about it. Who would you rather buy from, a salesperson or a friend?

Try this experiment. Say you want to sell light bulbs over the phone as a fund-raiser for homeless children. You call people and say (reading from your script), "Studies show that light bulbs burn out once a month. You can buy several from me right now and help the kids in your neighborhood, as well. How many do you want?"

If you make enough calls you will make a few sales. The law of averages is on your side. You will always sell the bulbs to *somebody* if you persist. That's why many companies continue using the script-sales method. It seems to work. The truth is that *any* sales method will seem to work if you stick with it. There is always *somebody* out there who wants your service.

But what else is possible?

What if you called someone and said (speaking from your heart and not from a script), "Hi, this is Mary and I know I'm interrupting your day. Could I talk to you for a moment about a service we offer that I believe will benefit you and our community?"

How would you respond to that type of call versus the first? Was the first call dry and life-less? Was the second caller sincere and friendly?

The key to success in telemarketing is being creative in the way you serve people. You must honestly want to serve the customer. You may not always make a sale, but that customer will remember you. He or she may even call *you* the next time a bulb is needed!

Do you see what I'm getting at? People do not want to hear memorized sales pitches. Your sales routine may serve you, but it does not serve your customer!

You can test all of what I'm saying in your own experience. Would you rather talk to a person or a machine? When you need a doctor, do you want to call the clinic and be diagnosed by a computer or do you want to talk to a human nurse or doctor? How do you feel about answering machines? Do you ever hang-up on computerized sales calls?

Know the benefits your product or service has to offer the customer. Then make your call and *be sincere.* If you know what you have for the customer, and you know the benefits for the customer, then you can trust yourself to convey that information in a friendly way. You might even try this: Pretend the person on the other end of the phone is your mother, or a dear brother or sister. *Then* talk about your service.

If you keep in mind the idea that you want to serve the person you are calling, it will transform your call. *Try it!*

SERVICE TOOL #7

Remember: The joy in business comes from *serving* people, not *selling* them.

Chapter Eight

YOUR PERSONAL SIGNATURE

or

How to Give Extraordinary Service

*"Human service is the highest form of
self-interest for the person who
serves."*

— *Elbert Hubbard*

What is extraordinary service?
* Extraordinary service is when a customer has a 100% positive experience with your service.
* Extraordinary service is when *every* Moment of Truth is managed.
* Extraordinary service is when the service is impeccable and obvious.
* Extraordinary service is when the customer feels so good about the experience he looks forward to having it again.

Here is an example: Joe Vitale, my coauthor, says Ad-Lib Publications in Iowa gives extraordinary service. Why is Ad-Lib so special? From the moment you receive their catalog to the moment you take possession of the ordered product, every step in the service cycle is flawless. Ad-Lib's catalogs are high-quality items that are inviting to look at and read. The catalogs are also easy to order from. Most companies deliver within one to eight weeks; Ad-Lib fills your order the moment they receive it. If you call, they are friendly and ready to serve. They have computerized files so if you are a previous customer *they know you*!

Clearly Ad-Lib offers extraordinary service. What if they make a mistake on an order? Does that mean they are no longer extraordinary? It depends. If they don't clean up their mistake, then they are no longer extraordinary. But if they offer *more than what you would expect* in order to correct the error, then they are delivering extraordinary service once again. *That* is a secret that will help you satisfy customer complaints.

If a customer says he ordered white paint and you delivered red. What then? I suggest you ask the customer what *he* would like to see happen. Then you deliver more than the customer expects. You might have to pitch in *two* buckets of white paint to be extraordinary to that customer, but wouldn't it be worth it?

Recently my family and I were flying to Denver on a skiing trip. Our flight continued to be postponed, and finally cancelled. We had waited a long time and were now stuck. At this point the airline was no longer providing extraordinary service. *But* do you know what they did? They not only gave my crew of five *free* round-trip tickets for future travel to anywhere in the country, they also booked us on the next available flight! Because Continental Airlines gave more than I ever expected, their service was extraordinary.

Extraordinary service occurs when there is *total* satisfaction from the customer's point of view. Extraordinary service is impeccable...service beyond 100% of the customer's expectations. As Tom Peters, author of *In Search of Excellence*, said in a recent talk, "You have to provide legendary service to delight your customers. Best service is no longer good enough."

YOU TAKE IT FOR GRANTED

Do you realize that we often take extraordinary service for granted?

Unless we are *told* that service is extraordinary, we often do not recognize it. Think about all the trips you've made on commercial airlines. Every time you travel you expect the airline to provide your luggage upon arrival at your destination. If the airline loses your bags, you have a fit. Right?

Do you realize that getting your bags on the right plane is no small miracle? You pick up your ticket at the counter and drop off your bags. Before you can check in at the gate, your bags are already on board. The bags get there before you do. Clerks and attendants move with precision to insure your luggage gets to the right place. For them, every flight is crucial. You and I take this mammoth service for granted.

Why *don't* we consider that extraordinary?

Think about banks for a moment. Every month you make deposits, withdrawals and write checks. Every month you receive a statement and possibly an interest check. Every month it arrives right at the first of the month. Did you ever consider what a monster it must be to keep all your transactions separate from everyone else's? Many banks handle over 500,000 transactions a *day*! It is a miracle banks are as efficient as they are. Yet *we* take them for granted. We don't thank them or *think* of them until they drop the ball. Then we *demand* satisfaction.

Why *don't* we consider that extraordinary?

Let's not forget about fast food restaurants, either. I may consider them a convenience rather than a service, but I realize there is a lot of work going on behind the grill. It takes a lot of time, people and effort to create those little burgers. I seldom acknowledge that effort. Usually I get my burger and eat it. I never stop to realize that the empire behind the sandwich is composed of people from truck drivers to cooks. I don't pause to recognize that it takes extraordinary effort to make all those burgers and fries at *my* convenience.

Why *don't* we consider any of this extraordinary?

TELL 'EM!

I believe we need to be told we are getting extraordinary service before we will appreciate it.

In a Dallas seminar recently we were discussing extraordinary service. A McCannics branch manager was having difficulty finding something extraordinary to contribute. His programs were old hat to him. Someone asked about his "seasonal warranty." The manager had taken this service for granted, while everyone else in the room was in awe that he could warrant a heating or cooling system for the season at a cost of only $40. The seminar participants had never heard of any other company offering such a program. The manager had failed to appreciate his own extraordinary service because he had not told anyone---even himself---that he had it!

Often people do not realize what they are getting unless you verbalize it. That is why banks and airlines go unappreciated for their great service. We have to be told we are receiving great service before we recognize it ourselves.

I am not suggesting you boast about your work. What I *am* suggesting is that you should not expect someone's acknowledgement of your service unless you first recognize it yourself. I bet you are providing a service everyone takes for granted, including yourself, that is in reality *extraordinary*. What is that service? Can you tell me? Can you tell your customers?

Most repairmen can fix the machines they work on, but if in addition he does not inform the customer, then the customer will never know to appreciate that service. What if the repairman had a "seasonal" warranty on his work and never told anybody? Wouldn't it be pointless? The customer would never know what a bargain he had!

Be proud of your service and share your pride.

PERSONAL SIGNATURE

There is a way to increase service recognition while increasing your ability to give extraordinary service. It is *so* simple. All you have to do is start signing everything you do.

To illustrate, let's assume you are a payroll clerk. What if the check read "Prepared by ___*(your name)*___"? You would realize that you are responsible for that check. Your customer would realize who performed the excellent service in creating that check. Would knowing these facts make a difference in how you prepared those checks?

Let's take it further. What if you bought an airplane ticket and right there beside your flight number was "The pilot responsible for this flight is ___*(his name)*___"? Would you feel differently about the flight? Would the pilot want to do the best possible job in taking charge of that flight?

I am *not* suggesting that you put your name on your work *after* you do it. That would be too safe. You could do a lousy job and leave your name off for your own protection. Joe Vitale once worked for a large oil company. The managers there wanted employees to sign their work, much like an artist would sign a painting. The oil company, however, implemented this procedure so the executives would know who to blame if the job was poorly done.

I suggest that you sign your name to your work *before* you do it. This simple act would make you very aware of the fact that you are about to give someone a service. Acknowledging your personal involvement will increase your ability to choose to provide excellent service. If you realize you have an opportunity to offer great service, you will more likely choose to do your personal best.

I recall a quaint hotel restaurant in Salzburg, Austria called Maria-Theresien-Schlo̊fse. The couple who owned the hotel introduced themselves to Susan (my wife) and me as being there to serve our needs. The husband was a great chef and before we ordered dinner he talked to us about the food. He was committed to our exquisite meal before it was ever prepared. At the end of the evening he solicited our opinions and thanked us for letting him serve us. Clearly his signature was on the meal. Susan and I will never forget the romantic environment of that evening and the joy of being served.

Now let's bring this closer to home. If you are a bank teller, all your transactions can say "Transaction by ___*your name*___ ." Most banks require tellers to place their initials on their work. I can never tell who does what, so the initials mean nothing to me. Identification is obviously required so the bank can determine who is responsible when an error is detected. What if the teller's full-name were required on every transaction? What would change? Would you take greater pride in your work? Would your customers get to know you better and possibly request you to handle their transactions?

If you are a nurse, perhaps you can put a sign by your patient's bed that says something like "Cared for by ___*(your name)*___ ."

An auto mechanic could put his card in every car he repaired. It might read "This car cared for by ___*(your name)*___ ." Most auto repair shops are set up so you never get to speak to the mechanic. You drop your car off in the morning and pay for it at a window in the evening. Would we feel differently---and would the mechanic do a better job---if his personal signature appeared on his work?

If you are a typist you might put a sticker on all your work that reads, "Prepared by ___*(your name)*___ ."

Putting your name on your work is powerful. It touches something deep in you. That commitment touches everyone who sees your work and your name. In a way your personal signature is a declaration of your desire to give excellent service. It is also an advertisement letting everyone know they are getting outstanding service. As we already learned, unless we declare our service as being extraordinary, it won't be recognized as such.

Many corporate executives are getting in front of television cameras, doing commercials that state their personal commitment to service. Lee Iacocca, for example, has committed Chrysler to "A Customer Bill of Rights." Bill Patton, Jr., President of MAI/BasicFour, puts this statement on everything he does: "There is nothing more important than our customers."

RANDALL'S

There is a wonderful chain of 40 grocery stores in Houston called Randall's. Randall's is obviously out to give legendary service. They have a booth in the middle of each store where a manager stands available to answer any question from shoppers or staff. Above him is a sign that reads "Manager on duty is ___(*his name*)___." *That* is a personal signature. That is one of the many reasons I (and 26% of Houston) buy groceries at Randall's.

Recently my wife came home from shopping at Randall's and discovered a small yellow slip of paper in one of the bags. It was the personal signature of the man who had sacked her groceries! (See illustration)

Dear Customer:
Your bags have been carefully sacked by

_____

I hope when your groceries arrive home you will find everything in good condition. If you are not completely satisfied with the manner in which your groceries have been packaged, please let me know by notifying my store manager.

Thank You

Another innovation Randall's implemented is to have their clerks stand at the beginning of their aisle as an invitation for service. This is phenomenal! It feels great! Clerks in most grocery stores stand beside their register until you notice them and push your cart into that lane. Clerks at Randall's step from behind their registers and walk to the beginning of the aisle to let you know they are available. You do not have to strain your neck and scan all the aisles to see which clerk has the shortest line. At Randall's the clerks are ready to serve. They are in fact *inviting* you to be served.

Years ago I escorted my daughter's kindergarten class on a tour of Randall's. Randall's now gives guided tours of their store so the customer can learn the nutritional value of every item on the shelf!

Robert Onstead, President of Randall's, says: "Managers must care about their employees, but even more important, is that employees care about employees. That caring will show to the customer."

It is clear to me that Randall's is a store with a goal of delivering extraordinary service. Their slogan restates this stand: "Randall's is your remarkable store."

THREE STEPS TO EXTRAORDINARY SERVICE

Providing extraordinary service involves three steps. They are:

1. *Inform people* of the availability of your service.

2. *Take personal responsibility* for the service.
3. *Tell people* they are receiving extraordinary service.

Are you an invitation to serve? You may not be in a position to stand out front and let your customers see that you are available. (Then again, maybe you can do that.) In some way, shape, or form are you letting people know that you are ready and willing to give service? Informing people of your availability is the first step in providing extraordinary service.

The second step is to take responsibility for the service you give. You can do this with your personal signature. Find a way to sign your work before you do it. This simple action can transform what you do, how you do it, and how people respond to what you do. Your personal signature is powerful. (Again, put your name on the work *before* you do it.)

Finally, let people know what they are receiving. This can be done in many ways. You will find ways to suit your situation. Banks could advertise their commitment to get statements out on time. Repair companies could inform customers of special warranties. How can *you* let people know they just received extraordinary service? Answer that question and you'll fulfill the last of the three steps to becoming extraordinary.

Again, the three steps to extraordinary service are:

1. *Invite people* to use your service. (Be an invitation.)

2. Put your *personal signature* on your service. (Take responsibility.)

3. Somehow let people know *they just got* your service.

SERVICE TOOL #8

Remember: People don't recognize excellent service unless you tell them to look for it!

Chapter Nine

YOUR INVITATION TO SERVE

or

How to Begin Serving

"For a long time it had seemed to me that life was about to begin---real life. But there was always some obstacle in the way, something to be got through first, some unfinished business, time still to be served, a debt to be paid. Then life would begin.   At last it dawned on me that these obstacles <u>were</u> my life."

--Alfred D'Souza

I believe serving each other is our mission, our purpose, for existence. Serving people can do everything from increase your well-being on the job to increase your profits on payday.

Service will ultimately bring peace to the planet. That is my personal belief. Why? Because you don't want to hurt anyone who serves you. If we become a world of servers, we will become a world at peace. As Albert Schweitzer said, "There is no higher religion than human service. To work for the common good is the greatest creed."

How do you become a better server? How do you let the world know you are an ambassador for service excellence?

There are five steps to the business service dance:

1. *Begin*: Commit to providing better service.
2. *Recognize*: Acknowledge service wherever you recognize it.
3. *Speak*: Communicate your feelings.
4. *Act*: Create a plan and take action.
5. *Enroll* : Invite others into service.

Let's look at each step:

COMMIT TO HAVING SOMETHING BETTER

What is a commitment? A commitment is a written or spoken declaration. Just as starting an engine is the beginning of a journey, commitment is the beginning of your transformation to service. Declare "I experience joy when I serve and allow service!" and you will begin the process to have just that.

Years ago McCannics' corporate office experienced what I felt was a terrible turn-over rate. People were looking for other employment their first day on the job. I hired a consultant to conduct exit interviews. He confirmed my concern. People were saying, "Too much is expected of me," "I don't feel accepted by others," "Nobody cares here," "Managers don't listen to me," and so on.

These complaints were inconsistent with what McCannics stood for. I talked over the problem with my board. An understanding friend confronted me with an alternative. He said, "Why don't you declare that there *isn't* a turn-over problem?"

How could *that* help? The problem wasn't with me, it was with them---with the employees who complained and quit. But I knew that my opinion could affect my staff. I met with all employees and acknowledged that though several people left McCannics, a great many loyal people chose to stay. Based on that fact, we really didn't have a turn-over problem at all.

It soon became obvious that I had acknowledged the uncommitted people who quit, rather than the caring, serving people who stayed.

Another example of commitment is Babe Ruth. His declaration of intent is legendary. He would point to a back fence and say, "The ball will go there." Then he'd smack the baseball over that very fence and out of the park!

Your word has power. Use that power to declare your intention. Everyone has ideas. Put your ideas into *action* and you can change the world. The first action you can take right now is to declare your intention to give excellent service.

ACKNOWLEDGE SERVICE WHERE YOU SEE IT

Start looking for opportunities to serve. Start noticing when you are served. Acknowledge service whenever you see it. Become aware of all the ways you are being served.

Do you realize you are being served right now? The whole world is serving you and you may not know it! Your spouse serves you. Your boss serves you. Your clients, customers and co-workers serve you. The gas attendant serves you. The postman serves you. The banker serves you. The police serve you. The electric company serves you---the list goes on and on! (This very book was written to serve you!)

Have you ever stopped to acknowledge all that service?

Just a short time ago I had to take a stand-by flight to get back to Houston. I wasn't mad at my secretary for failing to book me on an earlier flight. I wasn't angry at the airlines for making me wait. I was grateful for the airport, for the possibility of a flight, for the kindness of the clerks. And guess what happened? I got on the next flight to Houston! I was being served. I acknowledged it and thanked everyone for their kind service. My acknowledgment will encourage them to continue serving others as well.

Look for and acknowledge service.

COMMUNICATE HOW YOU FEEL

Once you begin to notice service, you will begin to have opinions about it. You might have complaints about what you see.

It is very important that you find a committed listener. You need to air your concerns, feelings and complaints. You need to share these with a person who will truly listen, possibly someone already enrolled in service excellence.

How do you find such a person? It's easier than you think. Servers are everywhere. They are teachers, speakers, ministers, policemen, nurses, lawyers, truck drivers, repair technicians, salespeople, clerks, cooks....the list goes on. Find a person who is an excellent server. Communicate your feelings about service to him.

It's important that you find someone who will listen without trying to change you. There are no right or wrong ways to serve. There are simply observations of actions. Share what you have seen with someone who will listen to you with total acceptance. In your act of sharing you will learn more about service.

CREATE A PLAN AND TAKE ACTION

You and I are creators. If you want something, declare your intention and go after it. If you want to create service excellence in whatever you do, map out a plan. Set up a structure that delivers service. Create the way.

What can you do to create service? Reading this book is the first step. What will your second step be? You might speak on service to a community organization. You might alter your habits at home or at work. I can't predict what might happen, but the possibilities are endless!

Outside my office is an atrium with plants and a walkway. While gazing out my window I asked myself, "What can I do to create service right there?" I decided I could put a bench out there with a coffee pot and a tray of cookies (my wife is an excellent cook). I could post a sign inviting the neighboring offices to stop by.

What could happen from that action? Just about anything! People will create relationships. Employees can serve others by bringing coffee and rolls back to their offices. People may start bringing food and sharing it. It could lead to a regular before-work breakfast or possibly an annual cook-off! (While rewriting this chapter I learned that a friend had done exactly what I have described in an atrium at Shell Oil in Houston.)

What can you do right now to create service?

ENROLL OTHERS IN SERVICE

The process begins with you, but it doesn't end there. You and I have to light the fires within the hearts of our fellow employees, family and friends. Part of that will naturally happen as people see the new you. They'll notice how you listen, how you deliver on your promises, how much happier and more productive you are, and they will catch the service fever from your example.

When I dedicated my life to service I began to talk about my mission. I told everyone who would stand still long enough that I was here to transform the world through service. Then I began to sponsor and host conferences on service excellence. I hosted these conferences around the country without charge. My goal was to spread the word about service. I decided if I must give away a conference *and* include a free lunch, then that is what I would do.

Now I have written this book on the joy of service. Why? Specifically to invite you and all your friends into service. To share the euphoria that accompanies serving. I want you to know that you can change your life, business, relationships and even the world, through service. Writing this book is my way of enrolling others in service.

I won't stop here. I will do more seminars, host more conferences, write more articles and even more books. I will create an audio tape series based on this book, and a video of my seminars on service. I will

95

continue to be available for interviews, on whatever media will hear me, so I can spread the conversation about service.

What can you do right now to enroll others in service? You don't have to write a book or host a seminar. You don't have to do what I or anyone else is doing, but you do have to do *something*! Whatever it is, commit to doing it and follow through!

Ideas to consider:

* Invite others to read this book.
* Open up conversations about service.
* Talk about the joy you experience in serving and being served.
* Support and acknowledge those who give extraordinary service.
* Ask others to join you in your commitment to delivering excellent service.
* Ask yourself, "What's possible? How can I better serve?"
* Ask your customers, "What can I do to serve you?"
* With everything you do, ask yourself, "Am I serving myself or my customers?"
* What can you do to give your customers memorable, unreasonable, legendary service? Make a list.

YOUR INVITATION

The joy of service is available to each of us. All you need to do to experience it is *begin serving*.

Service is a dance...a dance between you and whoever you serve, or between you and whoever serves you.

I've already started the music for the "Joy of Service" dance. I'm your first partner. This book is my service to you. In a sense, I am leading in this first dance and you are being served by these pages. Now it's *your* turn.

Reach out your hand and begin serving.

Welcome to the dance!

SERVICE TOOL #9

Remember: Acknowledge service
and
allow yourself to be served.

97

Joe Vitale's Afterword

Knowing Ron and co-creating this book with him has made me alert to service. I am now sensitive to how I am---and am not---served. And that is both a blessing and a curse.

Recently my wife and I were in a new supermarket. We were checking out when a woman behind us asked our clerk where the diapers were located. The clerk shrugged and said, "I don't know." She didn't try to help the customer. She was doing her job and nothing more. Whenever you think more of yourself than your customer, you aren't delivering service. That clerk was obviously thinking only of herself.

Seeing this kind of service is the curse of McCann's message. My wife would agree. We are now sensitized to such an extent that we notice service wherever we go. When it's poor service, we know it. We don't like it, either, because receiving uncaring service feels lousy. It's dehumanizing.

On the other hand, I have found wonderful service and incredible servers. While writing this book I had to call the offices of Nordstrom to get permission to use an excerpt from their employee manual (in chapter five). It took six long distance phone calls, but every time I spoke with a Nordstrom employee, I felt great. These Nordstrom folks didn't know me and will probably never meet me. I was a stranger on the phone making what could have been considered an oddball request. But those employees gave me excellent, even outstanding service. When I finally connected with John Nordstrom I told him what wonderful people he had working for him. "They're not working for me," he said. "They're working for you."

That is the blessing of Ron's message. Now, whenever you or I receive great service, we will know it and we will *feel* it. And it will feel *wonderful*!

Here's an example: I finished writing the above line when one of Ron's secretaries came into my office and asked if I wanted a cinnamon roll. I said sure, why not (even though there are plenty of reasons for why not). I started to get up when Kelly said, "I'll get it for you." I said that's okay. She said, "I'll put it on a plate and bring it to you." As she was going out the door she said, "I'll bring you more coffee, too."

Yes, receiving excellent service feels really nice.

Thank you, Ron. I am now able to accept and appreciate what I might once have taken for granted. As for the mediocre service I notice---that's okay too, because that means there is an opportunity for excellent service. And that is the reason we wrote this book.

How has Ron's message influenced my own delivery of service? Good question. What I do now is ask myself a basic question: "Am I doing everything I can for this customer?" If there's something else for me to say or do, something that would make my customers and clients feel really wonderful, then I go ahead and do it.

Why? Because I've learned that *giving* outstanding service feels just as great as getting it.

And there's no curse in that!

Joe Vitale

BIBLIOGRAPHY

Everyone is a Customer by Michale Joan Bandley and Elizabeth I. Kearney. (1987, Kearney/Bandley Enterprises)

The Customer is Key by Milind M. Lele with Jagdish N. Sheth. (1987, John Wiley & Sons, Inc.)

Service Management: Strategy and Leadership in Service Businesses by Richard Normann. (1984, John Wiley & Sons, Inc.)

The Complete Guide to Customer Service by Linda M. Lash. (1989, John Wiley & Sons, Inc.)

The Customer Connection: Quality for The Rest of Us by John Guaspari. (1988, American Management Association)

The Joy of Working by Denis Waitley and Reni L. Witt. (1986, Ballantine Books)

Service America! by Karl Albrecht and Ron Zemke. (1985, Dow Jones-Irwin)

How Can I Help? Stories and Reflections on Service by Ram Dass and Paul Gorman. (1985, Alfred A. Knopf)

Take This Job and Love It by Dennis T. Jaffe and Cynthia D. Scott. (1988, Fireside/Simon and Schuster)

Growing a Business by Paul Hawken.
(1988, Fireside/Simon & Schuster)

Honest Business by Michael Phillips and Salli Rasberry.
(1981, Random House)

How to Win Customers and Keep Them for Life by Michael LeBoeuf. (1989, Berkley)

Managing to Keep The Customer by Robert L. Desatnick.
(1987, Jossey-Bass Management Series)

At America's Service by Karl Albrecht and Ron Zemke.
(1988, Dow Jones-Irwin)

RESOURCES

For more information about Werner Erhard's "The Forum" (mentioned in the first chapter), write or call:

San Francisco Area Center
62 First Street
San Francisco, CA 94105
(415) 882-6300

For more information about Barry Neil Kaufman's work with autistic children (also in the first chapter), write or call:

The Option Institute
RD #1, Box 174-A
Sheffield, MA 01257
(413) 229-2100

ABOUT THE AUTHORS

Ron McCann is President of Service Management Systems, and McCannics Services. He has been in the business of delivering service over twenty years, beginning in 1967 as an employee in his father's air conditioning repair company.

After having a vision in church, and after experiencing many personal growth seminars, McCann devoted his life to service excellence. He is on a mission to inspire people to begin delivering legendary service. Through his popular seminars, workshops, and newsletters McCann teaches people that caring about fellow employees and customers brings a special joy that touches everyone.

For more information about the philosophy and work of Ron McCann, write or call:

Service Information Source Publications
10707 Corporate Drive, Suite 101
Stafford, Texas 77477
(713) 240-4040

Joe Vitale is the author of many publications, including the 1988 book, *Turbocharge Your Writing!*

Vitale has interviewed contractors who specialize in service and written articles about service for national magazines. He is the editor of *Serving You!*, the newsletter of Service Management Systems.

SERVICE TOOLS

#1 .　Serve for the *Joy* of serving!

#2.　Don't substitute convenience for service.

#3.　Inside every complaint is a request for service.

#4.　Manage your Moments of Truth and you will become irresistible.

#5.　Take care of your customers and invite your boss to take care of you.

#6.　Managers are not responsible for the *work* people do, but for the *people* who do the work.

#7.　The joy in business comes from *serving* people, not *selling* them.

#8.　People don't recognize excellent service unless you tell them to look for it!

#9.　Acknowledge service and allow yourself to be served.

Great Gifts for Family and Friends!

ORDER FORM

Please send me:

o   BOOK: **$10.95 each**
_____ copy(s) of THE JOY OF SERVICE!
by Ron McCann and Joe Vitale. (Quantity
discounts available for over 10 books.)

o   POSTER: **$ 2.00 each**
copy of the "Service Tools." (Suitable for framing.)

o   NEWSLETTER: **Free**
copy of SERVING YOU! (Service Management
Systems newsletter.)

o   SEMINARS, WORKSHOPS, CONFERENCES:
a schedule of Ron McCann's workshops, talks and
seminars.   **Free**

Name: _____

Company: _____

Address: _____

City/State/Zip: _____

Telephone: _____

Please make check payable to:

Service Information Source Publications
10707 Corporate Drive, Suite 101
Stafford, Texas 77477

Great Gifts for Family and Friends!

ORDER FORM

Please send me:

o   BOOK: **$10.95 each**
    _____ copy(s) of THE JOY OF SERVICE!
    by Ron McCann and Joe Vitale. (Quantity
    discounts available for over 10 books.)

o   POSTER: **$ 2.00 each**
    copy of the "Service Tools." (Suitable for framing.)

o   NEWSLETTER: **Free**
    copy of SERVING YOU! (Service Management
    Systems newsletter.)

o   SEMINARS, WORKSHOPS, CONFERENCES:
    a schedule of Ron McCann's workshops, talks and
    seminars.   **Free**

Name: _____

Company: _____

Address: _____

City/State/Zip: _____

Telephone: _____

Please make check payable to:

Service Information Source Publications
10707 Corporate Drive, Suite 101
Stafford, Texas 77477